To GREG!
Leading our children to PEACE is a GOAL For All of us!
God Bless —

Mike

The Art of Humane Living

The Art of Humane Living
Martial Arts as a Path to Peace©

Michael R. Foley, M.D.

Chaos
Publishing Co.

Copyright © 2004 by Michael R. Foley, M.D.

Published and distributed in the United States by:

Chaos Publishing Company

6570 N. Lost Dutchman Drive

Paradise Valley, Arizona 85253

Phone: 480-483-0242

Fax: 480-483-7605

Website: chaospublishing.com

Photos: Silvio Rone

Graphic/Book Design: Amy Craig

All rights reserved. No part of this book may be reproduced by any mechanical, photographic, or electronic process, or in the form of a phonographic recording; nor may it be stored in a retrieval system, transmitted, or otherwise copied for public or private use – other than for "fair use" as brief quotations embodied in articles and reviews without prior written permission of the publisher. The author of this book does not dispense medical advice or prescribe the use of any technique as a form of treatment for any physical, mental, or medical problem. The intent of the author is to only offer information of a general nature to help you in your quest for emotional and spiritual well-being and peace. In the event you use any of the information in this book for yourself, which is your constitutional right, the author and the publisher assume no responsibility for your actions.

Library of Congress Control Number: 2003114077

Foley, M.D., Michael R.

The Art of Humane Living/Martial Arts as a Path to Peace

ISBN 0-9745811-0-0+52995

1st Printing, April 27, 2004

Printed in China

For Lisa, Bonnie, Molly and Michael

Words of Gratitude

I am extremely indebted to everyone who made writing this book truly a "Path to Peace":

> To my friend Dr. Terrence Webster-Doyle for encouraging me to put my thoughts on paper.
>
> To my past teachers, Gabriel Vargas and Carl Clarizio, Jr., for the "Gift" of the Martial Arts.
>
> To my students and friends who assisted me with "sculpting" the messages within.
>
> To Silvio Rone and Amy Craig for their gentle manner and artistic brilliance in bringing life to my lessons with relationship photography and design.
>
> To Susan Weisman and Adryan Russ for their outstanding editorial assistance and good humor.
>
> To Sue Cho for her beautiful calligraphy that captures the "intent."
>
> To my mother Bette, my father Ray and my brother Jim for their guidance and love.
>
> To my core family: Lisa, Bonnie, Molly and Michael for their love, patience and encouragement. I love you all!

Thank you,
Sa Bum Nim Mike Foley
"Teacher of Peace"

평화
Peace

2001.4.28

아동들의 평화권

Contents

Foreword	14
Introduction	18
A Message to the Reader	22
Read this first: A Word to Our New Leaders	24
Read this second: Our Real Teachers	26
Section I. The Paradox: The Fight That Leads to Peace	**28**
Lesson 1: Living in the Moment	30
Lesson 2: The Paradox of the Martial Arts	34
Lesson 3: Creating Peace Begins Within	38
Section II. Respect: The Key That Unlocks the Paradox	**42**
Lesson 4: The Silent Message of the Bow	44
Lesson 5: Practicing Intelligent Martial Arts	48
Lesson 6: Focusing on Student Progress	52
Section III. Balance: Self-Discovery and Self-Control	**56**
Lesson 7: Learning to Combat in a Safe Environment	58
Lesson 8: Recognizing the Anger Trap	62
Lesson 9: Finding Refuge from the Storm	66
Lesson 10: The Source of Our Struggles	70
Section IV. Relationships: We Are What We Think	**74**
Lesson 11: Getting to Know One's Self	76
Lesson 12: The Challenge of Our Family	80

Contents

Lesson 13: Getting Along in the World ... 86

Lesson 14: Bonding with Our Environment ... 90

Section V. People Skills: The Path to Peace ... 94

Lesson 15: Breaking Boards and Breaking Free ... 96

Lesson 16: The Gift of Life Skills ... 100

Lesson 17: Martial Arts and the Family Unit ... 104

Lesson 18: The Power of Role-Play ... 110

Section VI. Success: Improved Self-Value and a Sense of Accomplishment ... 114

Lesson 19: The Value of the Empty Cup ... 116

Lesson 20: Chi Energy: The Life Force That Flows Through and Around Us ... 120

Lesson 21: The Real Cornerstones of Success ... 124

Section VII. The Bully: Our Key to Understanding ... 128

Lesson 22: Intuition: Our Best Self-Defense ... 130

Lesson 23: The Best Way to Fight a Bully ... 134

Lesson 24: Self-Esteem: The Most Powerful Weapon ... 140

Contents

Section VIII. Martial Arts:
The Shaping of Skills and Aptitudes — 144
   Lesson 25: Forms:
   The Art of Harmonizing the Hard with the Soft — 146
   Lesson 26: Competition:
   The Art of Graciously Winning and Losing — 150
   Lesson 27: Practice:
   The Art of Enjoying the Mundane — 154

Section IX. Discovery:
The Result of Personal Exploration and Development — 158
   Lesson 28: The Center of Our Being — 160
   Lesson 29: Accountability:
   The Core of Our Motivation and Spirit — 164
   Lesson 30: The Essence of Black Belt — 168

Section X. Power: We Are What We Can Imagine — 172
   Lesson 31: The Circle of Respect — 174
   Lesson 32: The Mastery of Creative Thinking — 178
   Lesson 33: The Path to Peace Begins with Kindness — 182

Foreword

At some point in your life – from your past, present or future – a confrontation will present itself to you. Not a verbal joust, or a fight over a parking space, but more likely than not, there will be a situation where pure physical force will be asked of you, or brought to bear against you. Unfortunately, in this day and age, people are of the mind that an aggressive and victorious show of force is somehow good, or right. If you take the time to read this book, really *read* this book, I think you will find that the opposite is truer than we ever knew.

I met Dr. Michael Foley about two years ago. My wife Shonda was pregnant with our fourth child, and the pregnancy was termed "high risk" by her attending physician due to a multitude of issues. Dr. Foley was recommended to us, not only as the best in our area, but one of the premiere physicians in the world in pre-natal care. I can remember walking into his office that first day. Upon shaking his hand and looking around, I was struck by two things.

First, his incredibly calm and friendly demeanor, and I don't mean a big smile and "How ya' doin'?" But more "Please, sit down and relax, I'm here to help." He made a very nervous and tense time in our lives immediately more calm and comfortable. The second thing that hit me was the display of Far Eastern culture in his office. We saw pictures of his family in karate poses and many trinkets I was sure weren't replicas. Based on what I thought I knew about martial arts from the Bruce Lee and Chuck Norris movies, these two things did not add up.

Our fourth child, Garrison Michael Schilling, was born on June 27, 2002, and his birth went off without a hitch. Garrison is now terrorizing us on a daily basis, spurred on by his two older brothers and older sister. To Dr. Foley I say thank you and God bless you for that.

As the 2002 season wound down, I kept thinking about a conversation I had once had with Mike regarding martial arts, and his program, Children's Path to Peace. Our oldest son Gehrig was at that uncomfortable age when it seemed that his every action and reaction were wrong, either to him or to us. We all know that Mom and Dad are always wrong – at least they were when I was growing up. I wanted Gehrig to have a strong male role model outside our home, someone who would afford him an outlet.

Some of the principles and ethics Dr. Foley spoke about regarding his program and how he teaches martial arts to children were the exact things I wanted my kids to hear – not only at home, but outside our home. In addition, aside from our kids, I was at a point in my career professionally when I wanted to expand my off-season conditioning program and had always had an interest in pursuing the martial arts.

I'll fast-forward about two years and tell you that the decisions made at the time were some of the best I think my wife and I have made regarding our children. The things they have begun to learn as they pursue the art of Tang Soo Do are things that would have been hard, almost impossible, to teach inside the home. We have watched Gehrig, and our daughter Gabriella mature in so many ways, and both of us beamed with pride when they received their first promotion, a uniform in Dr. Foley's class. Gehrig has since moved on and received his first belt promotion.

On a personal note, I can honestly tell you that the time Mike and I have spent as a student and teacher, friend with friend, have been some of the most rewarding and life-changing experiences I've ever had. I have also had the distinct pleasure of being taught by his incredible wife Lisa, as well as one of his top students, Lori Contreras. Each of them has presented me with situations and ideas that have changed who I am, how I think, and what I feel about myself, and about others.

When you get down to it, that is really what this book is about, how you feel about yourself, and once you find this out, realizing how significantly it affects how you feel about and treat other people. Okay, I won't lie to you. Learning to crush someone's Adam's apple wasn't a bad thing. I entered the arena of martial arts with a strong desire to become some sort of tough guy. But now that I have waded more deeply into the art, I realize that my true goal is to never let that tough guy be seen, unless, of course, my family's health or safety is at risk.

All of the things I thought were tough and manly in life, the things the newspapers and TV shows told me were tough – well, let's just say they are what they are, a media creation.

I will admit to not being the best student in the world. I still struggle on a daily basis to organize my life in a way a true master of the art can and does, the way Mike does; but it is something I will do one day. I will attain what is before me – of that I am sure. I will do it because of people like Mike Foley, people whose goal each day is to help others enjoy life as much as they do, people who look for any and every opportunity to make a positive difference in everyone's life. It's not lip service with the Foleys, it's a way of life.

This book you now hold in your hands is, at its core, Dr. Mike Foley. It's what he is, what he believes, what he wants for you, and all of it is good.

I am deeply honored to have been asked to write the foreword for this book, honored by the simple fact that someone – who's done more with life in a week than most do in a decade – would think enough of me to value my opinion of his work. If you really read this book, your life and the lives of those you care about will change, and all of that change will be for the better.

Thanks, Mike. God bless.

—Curt Schilling

Introduction

The Art of Humane Living: Martial Arts as a Path to Peace – is this title a contradiction, an oxymoron? How can the martial arts be a path to peace? And what do the martial arts have to do with humane living?

Among the many important things Dr. Foley asks us to consider in this new book is his perception that the martial arts can be a vehicle for getting along in the world – a means for self-understanding and social welfare. This paradox – that we can engage in a fight that leads to peace – is no small statement! If it is true, then this book is surely worth reading. Yet, to accept this vision, we need to put aside our old paradigm, our old patterns of belief – we must "empty our cup," empty our mind of the preconditioned view of the martial arts – the ones popularized by Hollywood as acts of extreme violence.

Through life experience, Dr. Foley's personal journey as a doctor and martial artist has brought him to the realization that the martial arts can in fact bring about peaceful behavior. Based on my 42 years in the martial arts, I can only agree. It IS possible. Yet, with this assertion comes a big IF! IF the martial arts can be taught as a means of self-understanding and not merely as a means of physical self-defense, then we have something unique and significant. What has conventionally been taught as a physical self-defense must now also be taught in a creative and transformative psychological context – so we use our minds in concert with our bodies. Do we need to be psychologists to learn it? Absolutely not! In this context, we are all explorers, hunting down the causes of violence within oneself and society, researching the roots of human behavior as well as the fundamental structure and nature of conflict.

Most people believe that the martial arts are about being able to defend oneself from a bully on the playground, or from an attacker in a dark alley. To a practical extent, they are. We cannot deny the danger that life provides us; people who harm others do exist. But what Dr. Foley is saying to us is that the martial arts can be much, much more! He is exploring with us how the martial arts can create an intelligent context for compassionate self-inquiry that gets to the roots of human violence – even end it – before it manifests further into long-lasting psychological or physical harm. He takes us through a collection of seemingly random insights into the causes of human conflict, using the martial arts as a non-judgmental mirror for self-examination and revelation.

Dr. Foley does not try to tell us what to think, how to act or what to do, which may disappoint readers looking for "answers." Instead, he constantly urges us to think, and then act appropriately. He takes the path of creative discontent by leading us time and again to examine, from moment-to-moment, our conditioned views of ourselves and each other, by using the martial arts to reflect our conditioned behavior. This ongoing self-confrontation, this continuous examination into the conditioned thinking that creates conflict in human relationship, helps the reader understand what prevents peace. In so doing, the reader is encouraged to put aside what creates conflict. In this process of creatively eliminating the "negative," one is then left with the "positive." We cannot *achieve* or *bring about* peace – but we can understand what prevents it. And in the very act of this understanding, the conflict that causes violence disappears. Peace emerges, naturally.

If you seek a typical panacea for peace, some new Asian philosophy to use to impress your friends or students, a new way of thinking to complement your existing conditioned views of the martial arts, or an intellectual viewpoint to debate, this book is not for you. If you are serious about understanding what creates human conflict, interested in learning whether the martial arts prescribed by Dr. Foley are a means to explore that conflict in a creative dialogue – if you are concerned about the terrible violence in the world and wonder if anything can address it intelligently – this book is for you. There are few books that can address an understanding of what prevents peace and what creates human conflict – via the practice of martial arts. This is one of them!

– Dr. Terrence Webster-Doyle, Martial Arts for Peace Institute

A Message to the Reader

The Art of Humane Living: Martial Arts as a Path to Peace© is a book about peaceful living. Yes, martial arts; yes, peaceful.

Despite the connotation that the martial arts carry of being a warrior's approach, they have utility and personal validity in day-to-day living. You may be surprised to discover that the teachings go far beyond the current conception of the martial arts, beyond the walls of the training hall, and possibly beyond your imagination regarding the kind of gentle power the martial arts can hold.

Although "martial arts" appears in the title and these words are used throughout the book, you will find that the concepts are universally applicable to all human beings, in every walk of life. The messages in this book are meant not only for martial artists, but for everyone – parents, teachers, students, doctors, lawyers, grocery clerks, bus drivers and CEOs.

The challenge for the reader is to look beyond the "programmed" thoughts you may have about the "martial arts" and to look toward the personally relevant message of "creating peace." You will find it in this book.

Read slowly and deliberately. Savor each chapter, and you will discover the art of humane living for yourself.

Read this first

A Word to Our New Leaders

Many years ago, just after the birth of my first child, my mission as a martial artist evolved dramatically. The responsibility of being a parent shifted my emphasis – and ultimately the importance of the art – from self-centered training to future-leader education. The gift I wanted all of our children to receive became the inherent discipline, confidence and self-esteem gleaned from a lifelong study of the martial arts.

My passion and my family's passion became the desire to pass on the wonders of the martial arts to whoever will listen. The world is so full of violence and hatred that we, as martial artists, must:

> Focus on understanding the human condition.

> Help our children understand and appreciate charity and compassion.

> Propagate awareness of prejudice and teach mutual respect.

> Emphasize the need for our children to pursue self-discovery and conceptual inquiry, which provide the tools for empathy and love.

Our future leaders must free themselves from the anchor of the ego and learn to value respect in all their relationships. When we teach our children to love and respect themselves, they can become capable of loving and respecting others.

As intelligent martial art training focuses on understanding the value of human relationships, it assists parents and teachers in shaping our future leaders. *The Art of Humane Living* reflects my passion for these intelligent martial arts. The messages conveyed come from my teachers, Gabriel Vargas, Carl Clarizio, Jr., Dr. Terrence Webster-Doyle; my family; my students; and my 37 years of experience in the martial arts. While the common perception of the martial arts is that they teach people how to be war-like, you may be pleased to discover how, paradoxically, intelligent training in the martial arts cultivates a kind and humane life.

The photos, words and concepts that you will see are meant to help you transcend the narrow application of martial arts to a more useful and universal application – the art of peaceful living.

Enjoy this book with your family and friends. Our future leaders are counting on you.

> While the common perception of the martial arts is that they teach people how to be war-like, you may be pleased to discover how, paradoxically, intelligent training in the martial arts cultivates a kind and humane life.

Read this second

Our Real Teachers

The true benefit of martial arts education is sometimes difficult to realize given the demand for insightful teachers, available opportunities, financial demands and realistic expectations. However, once the right teacher and environment are finally embraced, students have the opportunity to discover that there's more than one kind of learning. Here are three forms we recognize:

Direct Learning. Formal instruction provided by a teacher is usually direct and didactic. This process of teaching is an age-old Asian tradition, which embraces the dictum of, "I teach; you listen." This method clearly has value. It forms the foundation for current martial arts traditional education.

Indirect Learning. This kind of learning stems from a step outside the traditional paradigm. The teacher, in addition to using direct, didactic education, embarks on a process of involving all students in open communication – encouraging them to ask questions and investigate for themselves the validity of what they are taught. Dialogue between teacher and student becomes important for both participants. The student benefits from the knowledge passed on by the teacher and the respect arising from the personal attention and genuine interest shared in the interaction. The teacher is not only handsomely rewarded by the relationship that emerges, but also by enhanced skill and effectiveness as an educator.

Community Learning. The process of martial art education that ultimately becomes the most valuable to students is community learning. Environmental or community learning is provided by fellow students in the training hall. Many advanced martial artists will admit that their most valued lessons did not come from their chief instructor but from their fellow colleagues in training. The community relationships that develop among those who stress and strain together in the "trenches" are rich and long-lasting. The trust that emerges forges the metal of empathy, compassion, and personal and mutual respect – the true lessons of the martial arts.

True martial arts education is experienced and shared in the training hall with the persons to your left, your right, in front and behind. Your fellow students, as well as your instructors, are your teachers!

> True martial arts education is experienced and shared in the training hall with the persons to your left, your right, in front and behind. Your fellow students, as well as your instructors, are your teachers!

Section One

The Paradox

The Fight That Leads to Peace

Lesson One

Living in the Moment

At the beginning of each martial arts session, while everyone is socializing and preparing for class, I strike a large gong. This instrument emits a deeply toned resonance throughout the training hall. Students are aware that this tradition signifies to all participants that class is starting and it is time to line up and bow.

The symbolic ring and resonance of the gong reminds everyone to be present, to live in the moment, and to be attuned to the here and now.

But it is a summons beyond the bow. Allowing the gong to ring, as the Zen practitioners would say, represents a call to awaken. The bell's tone calls to each student to not only line up, but to wake up. Striking the gong, therefore, is a much deeper and more personally relevant call than just a cue to line up for class. The symbolic ring and resonance of the gong reminds everyone to be present, to live in the moment, and to be attuned to the here and now.

As the alarm clock in the morning beckons us to arise and start fresh and anew, this ringing-of-the-gong awakening reminds each student to forget about what has happened in the past, prior to class, to forget about what may happen in the future, what plans they may have after class, and to focus on being mentally present, right here and right now, for the experience at hand.

By clearing the mind and focusing only on the present, the subtle nuances of the training session take on a whole new and more enriching meaning:

- The environment is more fully discovered and appreciated.
- Learning becomes more fun and less pressure-filled.
- The focus truly becomes the process or the journey and not the end point or destination.
- As a result, class time blossoms into a time of self-discovery and personal development.

Learning to heed the call of the gong and to be present in the moment is a reminder that this call is a philosophy to be applied to life in general.

Being present and available during all interactions with other human beings will ultimately result in the development of richly rewarding relationships.

Being present and available during all interactions with other human beings will ultimately result in the development of richly rewarding relationships.

Listen, martial artists, to the wisdom of the resounding gong. Live every moment; be present with other human beings so that the richness of association with other people can touch your life. Yes, indeed! The gong means a lot more that just lining up.

Lesson Two

The Paradox of the Martial Arts

When we watch children play and interact "in the moment" during the very early years, we can appreciate their genuine innocence. As the perils of life mold and condition the personality, the loving kindness of a child can harden to a more calloused and less kind attitude toward others.

> In order to help our students reconnect with their child-like humanity, we must help them become aware of who they are and why they feel the way they do about certain individuals, places and emotions.

While being kind to other human beings is innate in our human makeup, we all go through circumstances that inspire us to be less than kind. Those who are able to endure negative life changes and remain kind-hearted, giving individuals – they are the ones who tend to be balanced and centered people who, like children, know how to live in the moment. That's why it's essential for us to remind one another of the importance of the "beginner's mind."

In order to help our students reconnect with their child-like humanity, we must help them become aware of who they are and why they feel the way they do about certain individuals, places and emotions.

Once students discover and become aware of how their "conditioning" may have a negative impact on their willingness to be kind and charitable, they can personally experience what may be preventing them from being kind. Whenever I ask my students what kindness means to them, the responses are numerous and varied. In addition to their own perspectives, the important concept I hope to convey is that kindness to all living things is essential.

As an instructor, I know that kindness must be inherent in my training and teaching. For me, kindness is teaching with passion, giving to the students' lessons of body, mind and spirit without expectation. A possible reward is that our students will also become teachers and give to their students.

All of us must strive to be kind and to discover within ourselves what keeps us from being a child of charity, and from living in the moment.

Martial arts education, if approached intelligently, results in kindness and love.

> This is the paradox of the martial arts. We learn how to punch and kick, but our first goal is to become kind, calm, peaceful.

This is the paradox of the martial arts. We learn how to punch and kick, but our first goal is to become kind, calm, peaceful.

Lesson Three

Creating Peace Begins Within

How does a martial artist create peace? The paradox of the martial arts is sometimes difficult to fully grasp as an observer, but once experienced, the participant understands completely.

> Self-discovery occurs when the root of one's own conflict is revealed.

In class, "martial skills" are taught and emphasized. When a student's personal conflict situation comes to the fore – as a result of practicing martial skills – students begin to discover who they are, what motivates them, why they have fears, and how to cope with their newly discovered "self." Self-discovery occurs when the root of one's own conflict is revealed.

A new sense of self-confidence and esteem develops as these skills evolve. This new confidence inspires a sense of calm, which becomes rooted in the individual. Students learn what to do and how to cope with the way their bodies react to sometimes crippling feelings.

Students learn to control their fear and anxiety in such a way that, in the face of stress, causes them to react differently. They *act* from confidence rather than *react* from fear.

Students become accustomed to their emotions and fears. As a result, they develop improved self-control and exude calmness in the face of adversity. They become peacemakers because they learn how to become a calming force in the storm of conflict.

The paradox – studying and training in martial or warlike arts, in an effort to create peace – is a learned process. Self-control, understanding, and realization emerge, enabling students to permeate calmness and become, not warriors, but peacemakers. As confident and loving individuals, they have nothing to prove and no egos they must defend. They have the power to control but they choose avoidance, the true definition of humility. The ultimate victory or success for trained martial artists is the ability to avoid a battle – to stop it before it begins.

> Students learn to control their fear and anxiety in such a way that, in the face of stress, causes them to react differently. They *act* from confidence rather than *react* from fear.

The ultimate victory or success for trained martial artists is the ability to avoid a battle – to stop it before it begins.

Section Two

Respect

The Key That Unlocks the Paradox

Lesson Four

The Silent Message of the Bow

In practicing martial arts, when we bow to someone, we outwardly demonstrate our respect by momentarily placing our head slightly lower than the head of the person we are honoring. By purposely positioning our head in this manner, we convey a message of our relative importance during the interaction. The silent message we share by bowing to another individual reflects our intent to say, "You are more important than I am."

The bow is the most important movement in the martial arts because it is the one physical action that wholly represents the intent of our training – to peacefully resolve conflict by understanding the importance of other human beings.

The tradition of the bow is revered among martial artists because it truly embodies our goal of "empty self" – the ability to live life without the negative influences of the ego. The bow, however, is often misunderstood and misinterpreted. There are those who believe that it reflects religious worship or praise to martial artists of the past. This could not be further from the truth.

The bow is simple; it is a pure demonstration of human respect; nothing more, and nothing less. The bow is the most important movement in the martial arts because it is the one physical action that wholly represents the intent of our training – to peacefully resolve conflict by understanding the importance of other human beings.

By bowing, we demonstrate the true meaning of respect. By showing others that we perceive them as more important than we are, we honor them and love them. Clearly this is good for everyone, both the person bowing and the recipient of the bow. With respect and love, the fire of conflict is extinguished, and peace emerges. Isn't it amazing that all of this can come from a simple but powerful movement?

Learn to bow! Show your students and teachers who is important and who is respected.

Learn to bow! Show your students and teachers who is important and who is respected.

Lesson Five

Practicing Intelligent Martial Arts

I can remember, during the very early years of my martial arts training, how the training hall was managed and how my instructor treated the students. Although he was a very kind and gentle person, and certainly extremely adept in the physical skills of the martial arts, something was missing. The classes were modeled after traditional Asian schools and handled in a somewhat militaristic manner when it came to instruction and student discipline.

Empowering students to ask questions and to test learned concepts for themselves, investigating their personal validity, should be at the forefront of our educational process.

The instructor stressed physical training and preparation for battle. He emphasized the development of "personal desensitization" to physical pain by making his students endure center punches to their abdomens and knuckle pushups. His world was conditioned by what he was taught and what he experienced as a student, and then as a chief instructor. He is a wonderful person and was an extremely caring and talented instructor, but now, 37 years later and an instructor in my own right, I have come to understand the value of my early years of training.

So much more is learned in a safe and communicative environment where students are encouraged to ask questions and investigate for themselves.

Although I have learned to appreciate the benefits of extremely rigorous training and the values of discipline and respect, in an environment where students were never allowed to speak directly to the chief instructor, I have only recently come to appreciate the concept of "intelligent martial arts." Intelligent martial arts emphasize the importance of self-discovery, motivation, insight, intuitive thinking, understanding conditioned thought, and self-mastery.

Empowering students to ask questions and to test learned concepts for themselves, investigating their personal validity, should be at the forefront of our educational process.

I certainly respect instructors who focus on the importance of battle, but instructors who teach their students to develop relationships with themselves and with the world around them do more. These instructors have tremendous talents to share. What I am suggesting is that instructors who teach the "Do" or "The Way" of relationships and life skills offer their students an immeasurable gift.

When looking for a martial arts school and instructor, I advise any student to look for a balance between "Jutsu" (battle techniques) and "Do" (the way of life).

So much more is learned in a safe and communicative environment where students are encouraged to ask questions and investigate for themselves.

Lesson Six

Focusing on Student Progress

Many students begin martial arts training very motivated. They come to every class – as if on a mission – to soak up every bit of information shared. They work extremely hard to learn new techniques, often staying after class to clarify or solidify their understanding.

> "Before the beginning of great brilliance, there must be chaos. Before a brilliant person begins something great, he or she must look foolish to the crowd." (Yunn Pann; Zis Studio, 1992)

Although the majority of these students progress steadily through the beginner ranks and are destined to be among the few who may eventually achieve the rank of Black Belt, something happens. At some point, in what seems like an instant, a handful of these students stop attending class. The once fervent push to learn dries up and blows away with the wind. Those students move on to the next chapter in their lives appreciating what they have learned in the martial arts but satisfied not to pursue further training.

What has happened here? Why have some of what appear to be your best students stopped training? Has the teacher become boring? Are the classes less interesting? Is the goal less attainable? In actuality, the process of martial arts education has, if anything, favorably evolved toward a more student-friendly environment.

Why do some students start, like thoroughbred racehorses, out in front, ready to win the race, then pull up lame and never finish?

The answer resides in the "on-a-mission" student. Patience, perseverance and self-discipline may give way to this student's need for ongoing progress. Without the reinforcement of continued physical progress, students, on occasion, will hit a learning plateau. Impatient students quit training and move on to another activity unable to appreciate the value that plateau-learning offers those who persevere.

In comparison, the "sideline" students begin their martial arts training far less conspicuously than the students on a mission. These students often give the teacher the impression that they are not truly invested in learning. They attend class irregularly and infrequently. They are quiet, soft-spoken and intent on not being the center of attention. When they participate in class, however, they do so with utmost sincerity. Their questions and concerns are genuine.

At the onset, their physical skills and self-confidence often lag behind those of others in class. These students experience gradual but persistent progress as time passes. They are slow to be promoted but when it comes to achieving rank advancement, they are generally deserving and delighted. These students keep hanging around. They are patient, self-disciplined, and perseverant. Their class attendance becomes more consistent as their confidence builds.

These students – like the tortoise who races the hare, and wins – have what it takes to succeed. They have the attitude and spirit to achieve Black Belt and become capable and compassionate teachers.

The lesson here is for the teacher. Be attentive to students on the sidelines. Reward those who persevere.

In the long run, the best students may not always be those who progress the fastest. Those who endure the process of training with slow but steady advancement truly appreciate how difficult it was to make ongoing progress in their training. They are aware of how hard they worked through plateaus to become competent and empathetic martial artists.

The I-Ching Kanji for the word "chaos" bears applicable wisdom for both teachers and students in this regard.

> "Before the beginning of great brilliance, there must be chaos. Before a brilliant person begins something great, he or she must look foolish to the crowd."
> (Yunn Pann; Zis Studio, 1992)

Reward those who have the courage to look foolish!

Section Three

Balance

Self-Discovery and Self-Control

Lesson Seven

Learning to Combat in a Safe Environment

Almost without exception, the most difficult aspect of martial arts training is overcoming the fear generated by going "toe to toe" with another human being. This fear is the reason many individuals stop training or never enroll in the first place. There is something inherent, an imbalance in one's harmony, that emerges with the mere suggestion of physical confrontation, even under the most controlled of circumstances.

Although they may bring their child to class out of their own fear for their child's well-being in our violent society, many parents will be upset and remove their child from class based on their perception that the instructors are unnecessarily propagating a "killer instinct." It is an unfortunate reality that many martial arts schools and instructors disproportionately emphasize the physical skills of fighting over the philosophical approaches to the art.

In intelligent martial arts, students focus on self-discovery, enabling them to overcome their most deeply seated fears without an unnecessary emphasis on fighting.

Inherent in the term "martial" is a defined and structured war-like art. This sometimes sways instructors to focus on physical skills. The approach that teachers take with students either creates a firmly rooted respect for the physical and technical aspects of the art or propagates an uncontrolled, unbalanced environment, inappropriately focused on fighting and competition. The balance is in the emphasis.

Learning to combat another individual in a controlled and safe environment forces self-discovery and self-control.

The psychological and physiologic responses one must endure, in a time of battle, surface as the fear that must be conquered. The battle here is not with the opponent but within the psyche of the individual. With practice, students embrace this perceived fear and discover individually how they can control it.

An "awareness" of the fear response occurs – seeing it, recognizing it, accepting it as a natural human response, and then controlling it – resulting in a welcomed "calm" that can be summoned in times of stress. Through practice, students become physically and mentally skilled and confident. As a result of this confidence, they acquire a unique ability to control their fear in a confrontation. They discover that they feel physically strong, which gives them the confidence to control the process of confrontation. Students discover that their strength lies more in their minds and less in their fists.

Their skills become so fine-tuned that they realize they have nothing to prove and no ego they must defend. Although trained as expert fighters, students demonstrate repeatedly that they choose to *not* fight.

Students have the power to physically control but they decide *not* to, because they have acquired a sense of humility – an understanding that, rather than one person winning, it's best when everyone wins.

The martial arts must be taught intelligently. The goal of the teacher is to integrate fighting skills with appropriate emphasis and to develop peaceful, humble, and confident students. To achieve this goal students will learn to fight, but only in safe and controlled environments.

Fighting is important and offers significant value in the training of martial artists. In the process of fighting, paradoxically, we learn the process of peace!

> Students discover that their strength lies more in their minds and less in their fists.

> Students have the power to physically control but they decide *not* to, because they have acquired a sense of humility – an understanding that, rather than one person winning, it's best when everyone wins.

Lesson Eight

Recognizing the Anger Trap

Integral to the training of intelligent martial artists is the concept, and ultimately the application, of effective anger management. We all encounter circumstances, processes and people that "push our buttons" and stimulate the physiologic reaction of "fight or flight" – where our fear causes us to either want to fight or run away. This intense survival mechanism adversely affects our ability to control our emotional response.

> Trained martial artists often take great pride in personal anger management skills. Eventually we come to identify our own value as people, as well as martial artists, by our ability to remain calm and in control, even under the most trying of circumstances.

Much to our dismay, anger may emerge and swell into out-of-control, intense rage and potentially regrettable behavior. Martial artists, through our training, learn strategies that help control anger from spinning out of control. As practitioners advance in rank and gain experience, we become more confident and gain significant self-esteem from our ability to control anger effectively.

Trained martial artists often take great pride in personal anger management skills. Eventually we come to identify our own value as people, as well as martial artists, by our ability to remain calm and in control, even under the most trying of circumstances.

We all believe that through years of martial arts training and breathing/meditation expertise we have become valuable educators in the area of conflict management. We begin to define ourselves by these beliefs. We see ourselves as living this role as a model for our students.

When we find ourselves in conflict, we often utilize the preservation of our own self-images as the primary motivator to avoid losing our tempers and being judged as hypocrites in our own cause. Herein resides the anger trap.

> The model for our students is to have and work toward a goal of peace, but only from a realistic perspective. We need to recognize our humanity!

Although the experienced martial artist may be skilled and committed to peacefully resolving conflict, self-induced internal turmoil may result from self-judgment as we compare our ideal selves with our actual selves.

This is human nature. As human beings, we are inherently fragile and imperfect. Despite superb training, the best of intentions, and genuine compassion, we all "lose it" once in a while. The anger trap will catch us regardless of how clever we think we are. We must pursue good works, empathy, mutual respect, sincerity, and human compassion, and do our best to avoid the trap of self-judgment and internal conflict that inevitably will "rear its ugly head" at times of human fragility.

The model for our students is to have and work toward a goal of peace, but only from a realistic perspective. We need to recognize our humanity!

Lesson Nine

Finding Refuge from the Storm

In children's martial arts classes, we teach a basic technique for self-defense that directs the children to raise their arms in front of their faces, like the bars of a cage, to provide safety from a frontal attack. In an effort to not advocate fighting and to support peaceful resolution of conflict, we call this a "safety stance" instead of the usual and more recognized "fighting stance."

> This radical change in focus results in a new *calm*. Inside this calm, there is a place for conscious thought and *insight*. Rather than experience uncontrolled anxiety, motivated by unconscious fear, a martial artist can *see* the vulnerability of an opponent and slowly and strategically plan the next move.

> When we take refuge in our "self," our mental strength reinforces our physical strength, and the synergy of this combination creates great power and understanding.

Children begin this drill in an apprehensive manner, fearful of being hit with a padded bat, later to discover that, with correct positioning, they begin to feel safe in the refuge of their "safety cage." After several attempts, they begin to relax and smiles begin to cross their faces.

A similar phenomenon occurs with adults when they begin "free sparring." At first they are fearful and, completely on the defensive, they attempt to block every attack. They appear nervous, anxious, frequently demonstrating misdirected strikes and hyper-energetic movements – analogous to what we call "a cricket in a hot pan." They jump around, flinging technique after technique without strategy or control, purely directed by the "fight or flight" fear response.

Adults, like children, learn to take refuge and begin to feel control in their "safety stance." As they become more comfortable, their excessive and unnecessary movements abate. Their focus moves from being purely defensive, trying to block each and every technique, to strategically studying their opponent. This radical change in focus results in a new *calm*. Inside this calm, there is a place for conscious thought and *insight*. Rather than experience uncontrolled anxiety, motivated by unconscious fear, a martial artist can *see* the vulnerability of an opponent and slowly and strategically plan the next move.

The pace of the action slows and strategic thought prevails. The intelligent martial artist discovers how physical control, brought on by the comfort and security of the safety stance, is analogous to the ability to take refuge in one's self-esteem and confidence during a verbal conflict. As the safety stance becomes a "port in the storm" for physical confrontation, conscious intelligent thought emerges, inspiring security in one's own self-esteem, self-confidence and self-love. What prevails is the conscious control of emotion during nonphysical confrontation.

Intelligent martial artists and teachers need to take the time to place emphasis on discovering the balance between the physical and mental contributions to this wonderful art. There is certainly more to be appreciated than punching and kicking. When we take refuge in our "self," our mental strength reinforces our physical strength, and the synergy of this combination creates great power and understanding.

Lesson Ten

The Source of Our Struggles

Why do human beings create and exist in conflict? There are many theories but one of the most rational is that "thinking" controls "attitude," and ultimately affects "behavior."

Our conditioning can create conflict inside us, which can result in our creating conflict outside us – with other people. Both kinds of conflict significantly influence our thought process and further conditioning. It's a wild and unruly cycle.

Thought
"Here's what I think."

Attitude
"Here's how I feel."

Behavior
"Here's how I behave."

Conscious and unconscious maladies in our thinking form the foundation for how conflict affects behavior. As human beings who control our thinking, why shouldn't we be able to exert more effective control over our attitudes and ultimately our behavior?

The answer is unclear but may relate to how the context or culture of our physical and emotional development impacts how we think. The phrase, "We are what we think" illustrates this point very well. The context of our development is the result of our family, environment, life experiences, and education. This is called our "psycho-social conditioning."

Conditioning clearly affects how we think and who we are. It is extremely powerful, especially when it is a result of our family, belief systems, traditions, and environment. Our conditioning can create conflict inside us, which can result in our creating conflict outside us – with other people. Both kinds of conflict significantly influence our thought process and further conditioning. It's a wild and unruly cycle.

Individual conditioning may adversely affect group thinking, which may lead to global conflict. Conditioning always begins with the individual. That's why our goal, as intelligent martial artists, is to actively investigate how it affects our thinking.

Awareness is the first step. Awareness leads to conscious thought and hopefully to the elimination of adverse conditioning in ourselves and in others.

Awareness is the first step. Awareness leads to conscious thought and hopefully to the elimination of adverse conditioning in ourselves and in others.

This adverse conditioning is what we mean when we say "that which prevents peace." When we are able to become "empty," we can free ourselves from the adverse conditioning that creates conflict. Conflict will not exist in emptiness or "no-oneness" (nothingness).

When we know how to prevent, resolve and manage conflict, using practiced skills in communication and relationship development – then we are practicing intelligent martial arts. Our thoughts create our attitudes and result in our behavior. We are in charge of our attitudes and our behavior because we are in charge of our thoughts.

Take control, martial artists! Become *aware* of the conditioning in yourself and in others. Create peace with your intelligent mind.

Section Four

Relationships

We Are What We Think

Lesson Eleven

Getting to Know One's Self

The all-encompassing premise behind the martial arts is to peacefully resolve conflict. In the famous words of Gishin Funakoshi, "The greatest victory is the avoidance of battle."

> The utility of a cup comes from its emptiness. Only in that void does its purpose emerge.

Learning to punch and kick do little to provide the necessary skills to prevent conflict from escalating to violence. The fundamental teachings of the martial arts, therefore, must center upon skillful appreciation for and development of relationships.

Learning to value the importance of our primary, essential relationships is the focus of every intelligent martial artist. Relationship development relies on how we relate to our fellow human beings, and finally, to our environment – but always begins with the relationship we have with our individual self.

A relationship with our self is the most important of all relationships because it is the one from which all other relationships arise. We must first be committed to a loving and devoted relationship with our "self." Without this, we cannot give wholly of ourselves to a relationship with others. Intelligent martial arts help us understand who we are. We learn to appreciate and love ourselves – our faults as well as our strengths – completely and unconditionally. It isn't an egotistical value of ourselves, but a healthy, grounded understanding of our human value. Once we have come to this understanding, we can empty ourselves of ego-related, conditioned thinking, and give of ourselves to others. In order to be "nobody" to everyone else, we must first be "somebody" to ourselves.

> We must first be committed to a loving and devoted relationship with our "self." Without this, we cannot give wholly of ourselves to a relationship with others.

Being "nobody" or "empty" means putting other people first and making our own concerns second, so that our ego does not overshadow the relationship. In order to be "nobody" and therefore open and receptive, we must already have developed a firm personal foundation for self-confidence and self-esteem.

In other words, we must have learned to love who we are, "warts and all," before we can be "empty" – before we can become a void – to allow in the thoughts and actions of others. The utility of a cup comes from its emptiness. Only in that void does its purpose emerge.

Lesson Twelve

The Challenge of Our Family

As peaceful martial artists, we dedicate substantial energy to the concept of understanding the root causes of any conflict in everyday relationships. With education, training and practice we become skillful in dealing with bullies of any kind. We dedicate our practice to preventing, resolving and, if necessary, managing conflict. With the person on the street, we become quite adept at handling difficult interactions.

The biggest challenge we face is building and maintaining relationships with people close to us – our extended family.

For some reason unclear to all of us, we are far less effective in resolving conflict with our own "flesh and blood." There appears to be a self-imposed, overt vulnerability in our conflict management skills when our "opponent" is a family member.

On the scale of intensity and frequency, all of us experience far more challenging conflict in the home, with our extended family, than with any other people or in any other place in our lives. The unfortunate realization is that our competence and philosophy regarding conflict resolution, that works so well in the training hall and in other life circumstances, fails miserably in the confines of our own home where it is needed the most.

We need to recognize that our home provides the perfect camouflage for the conflict ambush. We never really anticipate that we will need our conflict management skill arsenal with our loved ones. An attack often occurs in a clandestine fashion. Without warning, conflict arises between our core family and our extended family. The attack is so swift that we are unprepared to appropriately respond in the way that we have been trained. Our humanity takes over and the cycle of anger, animosity, and grudge emerges without the moderation inherent in a trained martial artist.

The solution is awareness. We must be aware of this whole process and be ready to apply our skills in this new unanticipated arena. As with any relationship, extended family relationships require care and nurturing. Compassion, respect and empathy provide the nutrients for healthy development and growth.

Assumption or Expectation
"They should have known."

Perception
"They hurt me on purpose."

Conflict
"This is the only alternative."

Most conflict stems from our perception of problems rather than from the problems themselves. This is especially true in the family setting where assumption and perception rule the roost. Family members have expectations or make assumptions:

> That family member "should have known."
>
> "I shouldn't have to tell them something like that."

This type of interaction starts with an assumption or expectation, which is followed by a certain perception that concludes with conflict.

Family Communication:

1. First, *listen* to your family member's point of view.

2. Do your best to *understand* his or her perspective.

3. *Clarify* what you've heard to show your understanding.

4. *Validate* this person's intent.

5. *Then*, seek to be understood.

6. Share how *you* felt in the conflict situation.

7. *Respectfully ask* this person to stop this behavior.

This is typical of family communication in general. The techniques of "clarification," "validation" and "specific request" are typically ignored to combat perception problems like these.

The biggest challenge we face is in building and maintaining relationships with people close to us – our extended family.

The experienced martial artist needs to listen to the family member – first seek to understand. Then, as a respectful listener, "clarify" by verbalizing back to the family member what you heard that person say. Next "validate" the intent of his or her communication.

Then – after clarifying and validating that you've heard – then seek to be understood. Share with your family member how what was said and the intent behind it "make you feel." Finally, make a "specific request" of that person to cease the undesired action or behavior.

By following this approach to family relationship management, you have a much better chance of eliminating assumption and stripping away the misperception that resides in the heart of most family conflicts.

Wake up, martial artists! Do what you have been trained to do! Peacefully resolve conflict. Especially conflict that resides in your own family.

Lesson Thirteen

Getting Along in the World

Learning to develop successful relationships with our fellow human beings comes from a commitment to becoming emotionally available to other people. Real relationships, those that move beyond the superficial, develop between individuals who demonstrate emotional vulnerability during dialogue.

Learning to express compassion and empathy are primary tools for a peaceful existence.

Students learn that in human relationships, effective communication is based on three factors:

Tone of voice

Does the person speaking sound sad? Angry? Upset? Depressed? Crazed?

Body language

Is the person speaking relaxed? Hunched over? Does the person have an arched back? Clenched fists?

Word content

Are the words being spoken polite? Respectful? Couched in suspicion? Full of distrust?

The way someone says something is often far more important than what is actually communicated with words. Context can be more important than specific content.

During martial arts class, great emphasis and significant class time need to be devoted to teaching relationship development and effective communication. It is through these skills that we can become peacemakers.

When in conflict with other human beings, martial artists need to learn to focus on:

Understanding

Listen first!

Respect

Give a person the benefit of the doubt.

Empathy

Call on your insight to see this person as a fellow human being.

Understanding that you cannot attack "emptiness" or attack from "nothingness" helps you create peaceful relationships. If there is no wind in a sail, a sailboat cannot move. If there is

The way someone says something is often far more important than what is actually communicated with words. Context can be more important than specific content.

no anger inside you, you will not attack. Think about this, it will become clear!

Awareness of how conditioning affects us and others is the first step toward understanding the "why" of any conflict. As martial artists who are truly for peace, dedication to understanding conditioning, working to be empty of "self," and practicing effective, gracious communication are the stepping stones to success. Learning to express compassion and empathy are primary tools for a peaceful existence.

Practicing mutual respect facilitates the elimination of hatred and prejudice. Engaging these skills must be linked to our communication style and intent. Our goal always is to express a calmness of demeanor. This is how to be a peacemaker!

Lesson Fourteen

Bonding with Our Environment

To learn the importance of our environment, all you have to do is gaze at the vastness of the night sky, the power of the ocean, the majesty of the mountains, or the serenity of the desert. In the moment that you experience the grandeur of any natural wonder, the self vanishes. "You" are not there.

That's when you realize the relatively small place that "You" – or any one person – occupies in the scheme of things.

In that second, that brief time when we are overcome by the enormity of whatever natural wonder we behold, we become free of "self" and are "empty" to feel the emotion of the moment. This energy flows to us from nature – energizing our being with the flow of Chi energy.

Martial artists often practice outdoors, especially in places of natural beauty. This practice not only facilitates a stronger understanding of our relationship with the environment, but helps develop the process in which we learn to empty our self and "fill up" with more human, worldly experience. A healthy respect for, and communication with, our environment enriches our lives. Focus on the importance of all relationships! Enrich your life!

Section Five

People Skills

The Path to Peace

Lesson Fifteen

Breaking Boards and Breaking Free

Nothing is more stress-inducing to the beginning martial artist, with the possible exception of sparring, than being asked to slam your hand, foot or head through a stack of boards or bricks.

> To the martial artist of today, breaking represents far more than a showy demonstration of physical prowess.

The idea of risking unnecessary injuries seems to the casual observer to be absolutely ridiculous. Why would someone subject themselves to this?

Traditionally, breaking has played an important role in the conditioning and preparation of those studying hard-style martial arts. When that style of martial arts was studied, students would thrust their hands into buckets of sand in order to toughen them up. They would hit a wood plank wrapped with hemp (makiwara) repeatedly, to prepare their knuckles for the trauma of breaking boards or bricks. Teachers would ask students to demonstrate the fruits of their training by exhibiting the necessary power, speed, technique, and focus to accomplish a break worthy of their rank.

Breaking, forms and basics represent the foundation of the physical art. To the martial artist of today, breaking represents far more than a showy demonstration of physical prowess.

To trust your skills, training and confidence enough to slam a body part into an inanimate object requires significant mental preparation.

> What is breaking boards all about? Overcoming the fear of failure by breaking through the limitations imposed by self-doubt.

The mind becomes the obstacle to a successful break. The fear of failure, or of injury, becomes so powerful that it either prevents a student from attempting the break altogether, or attenuates the all-out effort needed to successfully accomplish the break. Breaking a board is well within the capabilities of most, if not all, students who have trained for even a short period of time in the martial arts. The objects to be broken, the bricks or the boards, represent one's self-doubt and fear.

The obstacle is the mind. If you believe you can't break, you won't. A successful break occurs when students have an unwavering confidence that they can. To the intelligent martial artist, breaking has value. Not as a flashy exhibition of physical skill, but as a metaphor for any obstacle that may be encountered in life.

What is breaking boards all about? Overcoming the fear of failure by breaking through the limitations imposed by self-doubt.

Breaking is far more of an obstacle to the mind than it is to the body. Break free, martial artists, and overcome the obstacles to your success!

Lesson Sixteen

The Gift of Life Skills

When new students begin training in our school, I make a bargain with them. My end of the bargain is that I will teach them martial arts, for free! I will give them the gift of my knowledge, wisdom and expertise; I will train them physically, mentally and spiritually. Their end of the bargain is two-fold. One, they must pursue training with passion and perseverance; and two, when they reach the rank of Black Belt, they too must give "the gift" of the martial arts to their students, free of charge.

I believe the martial arts must be viewed as a gift. The intent is that the gift will be passed on – from teacher to student – for generations to come.

The meaning of the gift is that something special is given away without expectation of reward. Those who have given "the gift" to their students will realize far more than they ever expected in return. Watching students grow and mature – exhibiting confidence and self-esteem as they pursue peaceful living – provides more than ample reward.

Those martial artists who make a living by teaching the martial arts require financial remuneration to pay their bills. They can give the gift of the martial arts by giving away far more than they charge. By teaching with passion and giving their students the value of "life skills" in return for simple class tuition, they have passed on the gift. They truly have given away something special without expectation of reward, by giving far more than they will receive in payment. They do this because the reward comes from watching their students flower into wonderful teachers and human beings.

The martial arts flourish because this teacher-to-student bargain forms the cornerstone of traditional teaching. Give the gift!

Lesson Seventeen

Martial Arts and the Family Unit

Most often a mother or father will bring a son or daughter to class for the first time because there is a perception that the martial arts will provide an avenue for improving a child's discipline and respect. In addition, many parents want to capitalize on the controlled environment of the training hall to provide for healthy venting of pent-up aggressive behaviors.

For me to realistically impart a long-lasting, life-altering message, I realized that I would need to educate the real source of my students' conditioning – their families.

Other parents, and increasingly so, are experiencing the aftermath of their children being bullied and want them to learn self-defense skills to protect against this social chastising. Whatever the reason, the child is often the first of the family to enroll in martial arts classes.

My efforts as a teacher have always been to focus on an elaborate education process, combining physical techniques with relationship skills, and role-playing. For approximately one to three hours per week, I have focused on teaching children the root causes of conflict and how adverse conditioning leads to prejudice and hatred. I have helped them use role-play to play out conflict situations, and showed them how to "use words, not fists" to successfully handle conflict. I have helped build their self-esteem and confidence by helping them master complicated physical techniques.

After several years of this method of teaching, a parent's comment changed my whole perspective and ultimately the focus of my teaching. The father of one of my formerly more rambunctious students asked to speak to me as he was picking his son up from a karate class. His son had been training with me for approximately two years and had made great strides in understanding bullying and conflict management. The father of the student said that he needed to relay to me what had happened to his son in the schoolyard that day.

This father began by telling me how wonderful he thought my school was and how he had trained, as a child, in Kempo Karate, making the rank of Green Belt. He commented on how his training had helped him as a young man, by giving him the tools to physically thwart advances from neighborhood bullies.

He then related how his son's response to a playground bully had surprised him. He said that his son was being picked on by a bully and the bully's friends on the playground just before school started. He told me his son was punched in the arm and that this scuffle was about to escalate into a full-scale fight when his son walked away telling them they were "too tough for him" and how he was "no match for them." This is a strategy he learned in class to deal with a bully's need to build ego and self-esteem.

As the father finished this story, I was expecting congratulations on teaching important life skills to his son. Instead he said, in a condescending tone, "What on earth are you teaching my son? I would have expected, with all the training he's had that he would have made short work of those boys. Instead, he cowers away!"

It was at this moment that what was missing in my teaching hit me like a ton of bricks. I was, of course, extremely proud of my young student and how he handled the bullies nonviolently. I later praised him for truly understanding that the greater victor is indeed the one who avoids the battle.

The problem I realized is that while I am able to favorably enhance a student's view on conflict and conditioning in one to three hours per week, this time-frame pales in comparison with the conditioning a student receives day in and day out with parents and family.

For me to realistically impart a long-lasting, life-altering message, I realized that I would need to educate the real source of my students' conditioning – their families.

From that moment on, my school, which until then had been limited to children, was opened to families. The fruits of this wisdom are now apparent for all to enjoy. Teaching the family unit reinforces the tenets both in the training hall and at home. Family passion emerges and new bonds, along a common martial arts goal, are created. Focus, my fellow martial artists, on the importance of the family!

Lesson Eighteen

The Power of Role-Play

As we have learned, one of the primary endeavors of intelligent martial arts is to teach proficient relationship development. The skills involved with the building, maintenance and management of relationships are not usually perceived by students and families as a primary focus of martial arts education.

> The whole process of self-defense involves learning about people and their behavioral conditioning. Self-defense is also about self-review and personal insight and how these influences affect personal communication.

Students, through a sometimes lengthy and often arduous process, discover that the martial arts are ultimately about people skills.

The whole process of self-defense involves learning about people and their behavioral conditioning. Self-defense is also about self-review and personal insight and how these influences affect personal communication.

Teaching students about constructive relationships includes sharing the importance of sincerity, empathy, openness and emotional vulnerability. These tenets, when truly understood by students, provide the basis for fruitful interpersonal relationships.

Learning to express sincerity and empathy while conveying the intent to be open and emotionally vulnerable is not an easy task. Through a process of open-forum role-playing, students come into immediate contact with how they respond to stress and social pressure.

> Through a process of open-forum role-playing, students come into immediate contact with how they respond to stress and social pressure.

Students discover that empathy and sincerity, no matter how deeply experienced, can be very difficult to convey via interpersonal communication. These skills reflect, like a mirror, on an individual's prior life experiences. Yet, students who continue to practice soon become cognizant of their inherent skills and deficits. Body language, facial expression, tone of voice and content become important areas of attention. Opening up personally and allowing vulnerability requires a certain controlled expression of ego.

As students learn important aspects of relationship-building, their participation in the designed role-plays, as well as their own observations and feedback by others, all solidify the validity of these skills.

The age-old adage "The way you practice is the way you will play" merits important consideration in role-playing. We always encourage students to practice verbal role-playing with as much passion and attention to detail as they apply to their physical and technical skills. What emerges from these new talents enriches the human condition.

The martial arts are wholly about people, relationships and creating peace. Play the role of peacemaker!

> As students learn important aspects of relationship-building, their participation in the designed role-plays, as well as their own observations and feedback by others, all solidify the validity of these skills.

Section Six

Success

Improved Self-Value and a Sense of Accomplishment

Lesson Nineteen

The Value of the Empty Cup

I am often asked, "Am I too old…?" or "Am I too young to start learning the martial arts?" The answer depends on the student. I have encountered open-minded 80-year-olds and closed-minded 8-year-olds. The more open-minded the student, the more likely that student will experience significant benefit.

> The intended message is that if your students enter a learning opportunity with a closed mind, filled with prior conditioned thought, any effort on your part to add content will spill over because of the already "full" mind of your students.

This brings to mind the age-old Zen parable of the empty cup. The pragmatic interpretation reveals that the value of a cup comes from its emptiness or its functionality in holding the intended content. Once full, there is no additional room for added content and, in fact, efforts to overfill will result in spill-over or lost content.

The intended message is that if your students enter a learning opportunity with a closed mind, filled with prior conditioned thought, any effort on your part to add content will spill over because of the already "full" mind of your students.

In other words, if your students think that they "know it all" from their prior life experiences or training, they will be difficult to teach since they will approach their training with "a full cup." This leaves the instructor little, if any, room to add content.

Therefore, it really doesn't matter how old or young your students may be. The paramount characteristic of a successful learner, whether in the martial arts or any life endeavor, is to approach learning with an empty cup.

> The paramount characteristic of a successful learner, whether in the martial arts or any life endeavor, is to approach learning with an empty cup.

Lesson Twenty

Chi Energy
(The Life Force That Flows Through and Around Us)

It's a widely accepted fact that improper flow through our bodies creates "dis-ease" leading to problems with our well-being. The proper flow of Chi, a life-giving energy, provides the right ambiance for health and vitality and the foundation for harmony in life.

Moving our Chi energy – by meditating on our process of breathing – brings health, focus, power, and harmony.

It's important for martial artists to have an understanding of how Chi energy moves through our bodies. Oriental medicine, based on this activity, focuses on alleviating the blocks in energy flow along the body's energy channels or meridians.

Moving our Chi energy – by meditating on our process of breathing – brings health, focus, power, and harmony.

Martial artists may use Chi energy for powerful breaking techniques or for establishing well-being and control.

Proper understanding comes from an awareness of how the breath is the driving force for Chi movement. By concentrating on moving our breath to our lower abdomen, following a slow inspiration, we learn to focus and move Chi energy. Experience with moving Chi in quiet meditation or during exercise allows martial artists to apply this life-giving energy to all aspects of their lives.

Keeping our energy centered, and maintaining harmony in the training hall and in life, focuses one's intent on health and happiness.

Keeping our energy centered, and maintaining harmony in the training hall and in life, focuses one's intent on health and happiness. Focus on the breath. Focus on life!

Lesson Twenty-One

The Real Cornerstones of Success

What are the greatest impediments to one's success? The answer resides in the realm of self-doubt and low self-esteem. The process of utilizing martial arts to improve self-esteem is by far the best utility of the art.

> Esteem and confidence are built and nurtured by overcoming the drive of one's ego to gain power.

Success is relative and cannot be measured by position, material possessions or stature in life. It is achieved by valuing one's self-worth and reducing self-doubt.

Negative judgments by others – as well as by one's self – are clear enemies to our self-worth. Esteem and confidence are built and nurtured by overcoming the drive of one's ego to gain power.

Since power has a strong potential to corrupt one's judgment of worth, overcoming this drive by keeping the ego in check will result in growth of esteem and confidence.

The rigors of martial arts training provide practitioners with visible and measurable changes in physical skills and mental control. This discipline leads to improved self-value and a sense of accomplishment.

The greatest reward comes from denying the ego and not using the new skills to "show off" and engage in battle. Instead, this learned self-control teaches us the art and the benefits of self-mastery.

Mastering one's ego, denying negative self-judgment, and relinquishing self-doubt are cornerstones for the foundation that the martial arts provide for improving self-value and, ultimately, life success. Believe in your self!

> Success is relative and cannot be measured by position, material possessions or stature in life. It is achieved by valuing one's self-worth and reducing self-doubt.

Mastering one's ego, denying negative self-judgment, and relinquishing self-doubt are cornerstones for the foundation that the martial arts provide for improving self-value and, ultimately, life success.

Section Seven

The Bully

Our Key to Understanding

Lesson Twenty-Two

Intuition
(Our Best Self-Defense)

Have you ever been in a social circumstance or new environment where something inside, an inner voice or gut feeling, made you feel uneasy and uncomfortable? Perhaps you had an intuitive, instinctual, or irrational perception that something or someone was threatening your well-being.

> This innate ability to understand or perceive a threat, without obvious or reasonable explanation, is intuition.

This inner guidance or intuition may have pushed you into a decision that intellectually seemed to be without reason but may have, wittingly or unwittingly, ended up saving your life or the life of a loved one.

Many people have experienced, or will experience, something like this at one time or another during their lives. Our mothers, for example, always seem to have an uncanny ability to know when we are hanging around the wrong people or environment. Advice to avoid these people or places seems irrational and unreasonable from our perspective but often proves, in the long run, to be potentially life- or career-saving.

This innate ability to understand or perceive a threat, without obvious or reasonable explanation, is intuition.

Intuition represents a high-level human survival mechanism that is a product of advanced evolutionary brain development. All human beings possess it and can tap into the protective benefits if we allow ourselves. The problem is that while we often hear the inner voice of our protective intuition, we rationalize or intellectualize why we should not listen to it.

> We, as martial artists and as human beings, must consistently access our intuition for self-preservation and defense. The way to do this is by being aware of our inner voice.

How many times have we had a bad feeling about going into a dark parking lot late at night, for example, but ignored that feeling because our intellect, or rational brain, told us that the feeling was illogical or unacceptable? The fact is that we put ourselves in danger when we suppress our intuition with our intellect.

We, as martial artists and as human beings, must consistently access our intuition for self-preservation and defense. The way to do this is by being aware of our inner voice.

We must not allow intellectual rationalization to interfere and put us into a situation that feels uncomfortable. Our gift of intuition is our first and most formidable method of self-defense. Listen to your intuition! It's there to protect you!

Lesson Twenty-Three

The Best Way to Fight a Bully

Can studying the martial arts reduce bullying? To an outside observer it would appear that the physical skills learned in martial arts training could be used to physically intimidate any would-be bully. Although this may be partially correct, there are many other more important considerations.

Training in the philosophical aspects of the art helps students to understand the causes of conflict both for themselves and for others.

The important understanding of psycho-social conditioning and how this shapes our ideas and beliefs helps students understand why most people who are bullies were once victims.

Understanding and being aware of the root causes of conflict allow students to enhance the picture with intelligence, which is often clouded by fear and intimidation. Once intelligence is tapped into, students know they can use words, and not fists, as their self-defense. Using awareness to prevent conflict is a very important initial step.

Verbal skills, body language skills – intelligent approaches to a bully, such as reasoning, cleverness, humor, and empathy – provide additional valuable tools for resolving conflict.

Ultimately students, if necessary, may have to apply physical self-defense measures to protect themselves from conflict, or manage a conflict situation that has already begun.

This intelligent approach to the martial arts fosters a better understanding of the three levels of conflict management:

Primary – Prevent conflict before it begins, through awareness.

Secondary – Resolve conflict, to prevent it from escalating.

Tertiary – Manage an already violent response.

The knowledge of "that which prevents peace" is more important and far more pragmatic in everyday life than the punching and kicking aspects of training.

The knowledge of "that which prevents peace" is more important and far more pragmatic in everyday life than the punching and kicking aspects of training.

Through role-play, students learn innovative approaches to help them deal with conflict and bullying. The methodology of these approaches must be emphasized and practiced in class.

Is a bully a bad person? The overwhelming response from the majority of young students is "Yes!" Most students will tell you that bullies are also mean.

In class, I present a story of a young man in a classroom who is clearly different from everyone else. I describe him as older, more physically mature – someone who wears black leather, has several tattoos and uses many swear words. I reveal that he has been held back and is now repeating the seventh grade. This student, who often pushes other students around and physically bullies them, has been involved in many fights after school.

I ask the students, "Are you sure that bullies are bad people?" The class is even more adamant, responding with an overwhelming "Yes!"

I continue the story with the bully's home situation. I let students know that the bully does not have a father. The father left the family when the boy was a baby and has never returned. The boy's mother was forced to work two shifts to support the family and is never at home. The bully has an older teenage sister who never speaks to him. She always has her boyfriend around and he picks on the bully, often punching and beating him up for fun.

This young man does not feel loved. He has no family support, no one to tuck him in at night, wash his clothes, make him dinner and remember his birthday.

I stop again and approach the class, "How many of you still think that bullies are bad people?"

The key to dealing successfully with bullies is to understand why they act the way they do. Doing things to help build their egos is a good way to defuse them. Bullies need attention.

The students now respond with sad faces, and they do not raise their hands. One student raises her hand and asks, "Why does the bully have to push everyone around and act so tough?" My response is that bullies are people too. They usually are not bad people, they are just responding to their environment and their own conditioning. Before they became bullies, they were victims.

Bullies are insecure and need to feel powerful. They need someone or something to build their ego and self-worth. By picking on people, they physically demand respect, which builds their ego. They need to do this because they are not getting respect in any other aspect of their lives, particularly at home.

The bully in the story has had a bad home situation and is a victim himself. Because he has no support or role model in the form of a caring family, he acts out at school playing the "tough guy" role to garner respect.

The key to dealing successfully with bullies is to understand why they act the way they do. Doing things to help build their egos is a good way to defuse them. Bullies need attention.

Using our intelligence to create alternative ways to build the self-esteem of a bully and prevent violence is the ultimate goal.

The class is now very well aware that bullies usually are not bad people. They understand that bullies often are people who are hurting inside and who need friendship and attention. The martial arts help us to understand that empathy and compassion may be powerful antidotes for the bully. Fight the bully with understanding!

Lesson Twenty-Four

Self-Esteem
(The Most Powerful Weapon)

Most of us, through life experiences, already understand that the way boys bully is quite different from the way girls bully. Boys are most often physical – they punch, push, pinch and physically intimidate. Girls usually don't use physical measures to bully. Girls most often bully by jeopardizing relationships.

Victims are made to feel that they don't "fit in" because they are not included. They believe they have to conform to the demands of the bullies in order to be included.

They are made to feel that they have to be someone other than who they really are in order to be accepted among their peers.

This type of radical peer pressure leads girls to inappropriate behavior, often jeopardizing their own health (drugs, sex, eating disorders).

They sometimes start vicious rumors, or have parties where certain girls are not invited. They create selective cliques or groups at lunch and practice other behaviors that tend to "include" some and "exclude" others. This is clandestine, sneaky and very hurtful.

Female bullies sometimes make fun of their victims and don't tell them why everyone is laughing at them. This type of behavior affects a victim's personal insecurities. The victim assumes that the bullies are laughing at some personal "defect," because she doesn't know why they are laughing. She then becomes hurt and depressed, feeling ostracized for what she believes are her personal frailties – her complexion, weight, class, grades, athletic ability or body habits.

This type of bullying is vicious and has lifelong implications. Victims are made to feel that they don't "fit in" because they are not included. They believe they have to conform to the demands of the bullies in order to be included.

They are made to feel that they have to be someone other than who they really are in order to be accepted among their peers. This type of radical peer pressure leads girls to inappropriate behavior, often jeopardizing their own health (drugs, sex, eating disorders).

Martial arts physical skills have limited benefit in this type of bullying. While mastering physical skills clearly improves confidence and can help these young women cope with the tactics of relationship bullying, the real advantage of martial arts appears to come from the self-esteem gleaned from relationships created in the training hall, which offers a "safe" environment where students can be who they are, without the need to conform to peer pressures of school.

Students discover that they are accepted and loved for being themselves. They begin to understand that a world of relationships with peers exists outside the school or classroom. In the training hall, they make friends and focus on a common goal.

The combination of learning physical skills to gain confidence, and mental skills to enhance relationships, in an environment of unconditional acceptance for who they are as individuals, provides students – boys and girls – the opportunity to cope successfully with bullying.

The instructor, therefore, is responsible for creating a culture (context) for student relationships to develop (content). Providing an organized rather than militaristic environment for learning and sharing is absolutely essential.

Students must be made to feel important – encouraged to ask questions openly and made to feel that they are actively participating in their martial arts education. This approach encourages ownership and helps create a mutual learning and teaching environment.

The martial arts class becomes a comfortable place where students are accepted for who they are without the need for façade. "Self-defense" emerges in the form of "self-esteem"!

> The combination of learning the physical skills to gain confidence, the mental skills to enhance relationships, and the environment of unconditional acceptance for who they are as individuals provides students – boys and girls – the opportunity to cope successfully with bullying.

> The martial arts class becomes a comfortable place where students are accepted for who they are without the need for façade. "Self-defense" emerges in the form of "self-esteem"!

Section Eight

Martial Arts

The Shaping of Skills and Aptitudes

Lesson Twenty-Five

Forms
(The Art of Harmonizing the Hard with the Soft)

Why do we practice forms? Simply stated, martial arts forms complete the balance of the hard and the soft, the yin and the yang. In contrast to the hardness of punching and kicking, forms provide an avenue for drama, self-expression, artistic performance and emotion.

While fighting represents the hard portion – the martial aspect, forms represent the soft portion – the arts aspect.

Forms are prearranged sequences of basic to advanced martial arts techniques that are performed in a traditional artistic pattern. The movements and patterns of the forms are seldom formally recorded. Forms were intended to be passed from teacher to student, personally, in the training hall as a valued tradition.

In older times, the practice of martial arts was forbidden by the ruling class of government in an effort to prevent common citizens from rebelling against the repressive laws of the times. Martial arts teachers would be imprisoned, and even put to death, for teaching or practicing. Martial arts, however, continued to flourish in the privacy of home training halls. The forms were taught to students as an individual way of privately practicing the basic techniques, while preserving a tradition richly ingrained in the teacher-student relationship.

Forms are performed in a traditional manner yet reflect the individual's artistic expression and personality. The hard must be balanced by the soft to achieve harmony. Express your individuality!

Lesson Twenty-Six

Competition
(The Art of Graciously Winning and Losing)

Competition and tournaments benefit developing martial artists. They provide an arena for coping with performance anxiety and learning sportsmanship, particularly when it comes to gracious winning and losing.

> Much of the American public views the best Karate teacher as the one who has the most tournament successes and displays the tallest and most numerous trophies in the training hall waiting area.

This graciousness, in and of itself, is an art worthy of focus. The benefits, however, while numerous, carry a cost. The same arena meant to teach sportsmanship may, and often does, backfire. Too many times the dictum, and ultimately the behavior, of "win at all costs" prevails. Students begin to view martial arts as another sporting event, an opportunity to win another trophy.

Parents and teachers often judge the progress of students by their successes or losses in tournaments.

Much of the American public views the best Karate teacher as the one who has the most tournament successes and displays the tallest and most numerous trophies in the training hall waiting area.

Excessive ego, fostered by tremendous tournament success, may paradoxically have an adverse effect on developing martial artists, making them overly confident and arrogant. Conversely, those who fail to achieve success in competition often conclude that they have "failed" based on feedback from families, coaches and teachers.

> Competition is good, but only after the core of a student's character has taken shape.

This is why the damage to the developing ego and self-esteem may be significant either when a student does or does not do well in competition. If, prior to establishing a solid foundation for self-confidence and self-esteem, damage is irreparably imposed, the true lesson of the competition is lost.

The real intent of martial arts is to contribute to the development of peaceful, intelligent and confident individuals.

The martial arts need to be viewed as a healthy way of life – an avenue for self-discovery, respect, patience, relationship building, and perseverance.

The emphasis for young students should be on these goals and not on a trophy. Once young students mature and embrace the true intent of the martial arts, healthy competition is certainly beneficial, but not until then.

Other methods of getting students to face their competitive fears can be created in the training hall. Teaching students to overcome the "fight or flight" of performance anxiety is important in all aspects of life, both inside and outside the training hall. Students go "toe to toe" in a safe environment of free sparring or perform a "solo" form in front of student judges, both of which simulate, in a real psycho-physiologic way, the same experience of overcoming the fears and anxieties of competing.

Competition is good, but only after the core of a student's character has taken shape.

The martial arts need to be viewed as a healthy way of life – an avenue for self-discovery, respect, patience, relationship building, and perseverance.

The emphasis for young students should be on these goals and not on a trophy.

Lesson Twenty-Seven

Practice
(The Art of Enjoying the Mundane)

Often in class, time is spent on what appears to be mundane repetition of basic techniques and drills. Practicing the simple basics frequently becomes boring to young students.

> The basics are the foundation on which the house of martial arts rests. If the foundation is weak, additional stories of growth and development cannot be added.

The basics are the foundation on which the house of martial arts rests. If the foundation is weak, additional stories of growth and development cannot be added.

During periods of mundane repetition, teachers must encourage students to explore the grand analogy of how martial arts teach us to live our lives and respond to conflict. The physical balance required to successfully perform basic techniques becomes learned. Students cannot advance in technique without practice. If unsure, students appear awkward, clumsy, unsteady, and off balance when challenged.

Students will discover that until they learn to keep themselves and their lives in balance, relationships, as well, will be difficult and awkward, resulting in conflict when obstacles are placed in the way.

> Students are encouraged to conceptualize even the most basic of physical techniques and apply the "balanced" analogy to other areas of their lives, especially relationships.

Students are encouraged to conceptualize even the most basic of physical techniques and apply the "balanced" analogy to other areas of their lives, especially relationships.

Once in balance, physical techniques are strong, and relationships are rewarding. Boring is good. Contemplate the mundane!

Section Nine

Discovery

The Result of Personal Exploration and Development

Lesson Twenty-Eight

The Center of Our Being

When performing a physical technique – any physical technique – students need to be encouraged to concentrate their "mind's eye" on the "one point" or *tan tien*. By putting our mind on this imaginary point, two finger-breadths below our navel, we bring our body's energy into balance. This process focuses the energy on the center of our being.

> The analogy of centeredness – being grounded and balanced, as applied to physical techniques – must also be applied to relationships and conflict.

The concept of centeredness is important for two reasons:

> For the proper execution and balance of physical techniques, such as the front snap kick; and

> For the process of developing and maintaining healthy relationships and balance in one's approach to conflict.

When centered, the body is grounded or rooted to the earth. Techniques can be executed with proper intent (non-aggressive) and therefore without overt physical evidence, or telegraphing of the attack. When out-of-balance or off-center, techniques are sloppy, approaches are awkward, targets are missed, and students are physically vulnerable. The analogy of centeredness – being grounded and balanced, as applied to physical techniques – must also be applied to relationships and conflict.

The martial arts are a way of living life. The concepts of balance and groundedness, while important for physical technique, are also used to define confident, calm individuals who enjoy life without taking themselves too seriously. Through the study of physical techniques and proper execution, students begin to understand the importance of being centered in all ways.

> The Martial Way or "Budo" is an example of how the value of what is performed in the "physical" has a perfect analogy in the "mental" or philosophical study of center, balance and grounding.

The Martial Way or "Budo" is an example of how the value of what is performed in the "physical" has a perfect analogy in the "mental" or philosophical study of center, balance and grounding.

The goal of every martial artist is to live life in balance, and to focus on the *tan tien* to create strong, physical techniques and grounded, enriching relationships. These concepts are what our students need to learn from the techniques that we teach them.

There is more to martial arts than the physical! Martial arts focus on life and its balance. Instructors must tie all of this together for their students. Find your center! Discover balance!

Lesson Twenty-Nine

Accountability
(The Core of Our Motivation and Spirit)

"Plateau learning" is a type of learning that occurs without a student's awareness. It happens while a student trains, without expectation of reward or advancement.

> What happens is that students feel alone within the art. They lose direction and often question their dedication to training. Ironically, during this phase, individuals may learn more about martial arts, and themselves, than during any other time of their training.

When students reach the rank of Black Belt, for example, or more particularly second- or third-degree Black Belt, they sometimes become poorly motivated for continued training. Until this point in their martial arts training, they have had specific goals to achieve rank advancement or learn new techniques or forms. Sometimes they reach a "plateau" where physical training becomes mundane or boring. Students become confused and feel that they have stopped learning.

What happens is that students feel alone within the art. They lose direction and often question their dedication to training. Ironically, during this phase, individuals may learn more about martial arts, and themselves, than during any other time of their training.

This is the point where an insightful instructor has an opportunity to help. Although students may believe that they are not learning, they are, in fact, being educated about motivation, attitude and spirit.

Those who become teachers discover that a deeper knowledge of the arts comes from having to be responsible for imparting the "wisdom of technique" to their students. "Accountability" for the success of their students becomes a new and less self-centered motivation for a teacher's continued self-development and training.

New teachers learn that the martial arts are not about them, but rather about their students!

For the first time, these teachers become responsible for contributing to the success of other individuals. The "self" disappears and the "I" and "Me" succumb to the "bright eyes" in the brand new uniforms, striving to learn. Motivation becomes fresh and less ego-centered.

Plateau learners now begin to understand that indeed they have learned more than ever. In fact, "the big picture" is finally revealed: The gift of the martial arts is there only to be given. Give the gift!

> For the first time, these teachers become responsible for contributing to the success of other individuals.
>
> The "self" disappears and the "I" and "Me" succumb to the "bright eyes" in the brand new uniforms, striving to learn. Motivation becomes fresh and less ego-centered.

Lesson Thirty

The Essence of Black Belt

Although encouraging student progress by way of rank advancement may appear regimented and structured, the focus of martial arts education is more a process of ensuring individual personal exploration and development than it is a reward for time put into a sport activity. Teachers, therefore, have the ultimate responsibility of deciding the appropriate gauge for promotion, based on a student's physical, mental and spiritual maturation in the art.

> From the very beginning of training, teachers must encourage and continually challenge students to look inward, beyond the physical, to discover their identity, their ego, their fears, and motivations.

> The skills of conflict management, empathy, kindness, compassion, and dedication to passing on the gift of the martial arts through teaching are the most important attributes of a true Sensei.

At the onset of training, students have an expectation for achievement and they set personal goals to learn the required kicks, blocks, punches and forms in order to receive the next, higher colored belt.

From the very beginning of training, teachers must encourage and continually challenge students to look inward, beyond the physical, to discover their identity, their ego, their fears, and motivations.

We have the important responsibility of attempting to balance our students' martial art development prior to rank promotion. This is no easy task, and one that should not be taken lightly. As students approach the rank of Black Belt, the duty of the teacher escalates from one of preparing students for another belt to one of mentoring a Sensei.

All students will have areas in their training where either they excel or need attention. Some will never achieve the physical prowess to perform a jump-spinning-hook-kick or break a stack of cinder blocks. This is where the personal development aspect of the art emerges as a clear priority for the developing Sensei.

The skills of conflict management, empathy, kindness, compassion, and dedication to passing on the gift of the martial arts through teaching are the most important attributes of a true Sensei.

The physical and technical aspects of the art are certainly important, and continued efforts to polish and perfect the "martial" or fighting component need to be modeled and encouraged. The authentic Sensei, however, focuses more on personal exploration and development and comparatively less on the physical.

Mentoring a Sensei is a period of discovery for both teacher and student. While students tend to focus on what they do poorly, teachers bring to students' consciousness what they do exceptionally well. The ultimate success for a teacher comes when students discover their own humanity and accept their flaws along with their gifts.

This discovery provides for the "beginner's mind" of the new Sensei. Students then acknowledge that the title of "Black Belt" or "Sensei" is nothing compared with the responsibility of "teacher." When students are able to put themselves and their egos second to that of their students, it is time for promotion to Sensei.

This concept of "Sensei mentoring" is best revealed by the actions of a senior Black Belt (Lori Contreras) just before her advancement to third - degree Black Belt. Prior to the promotion test, in which many of her students were testing for first-degree Black Belt, she requested that she not be tested that day. She made this request because she believed it was more important to remain on the sidelines, to provide emotional support for her students during their "big day."

She put the success of her students above her success, acting as a true Sensei. This demonstration of selflessness and accountability to her students made it very apparent that she was ready for promotion.

Mentoring students to progress physically, mentally, and spiritually to achieve the rank of Black Belt is wonderfully rewarding. Watching students strive, as Senseis, to ensure that their students achieve more than they do – as parents would for their own children – is truly the essence of what it means to be a Black Belt Sensei.

> Watching students strive, as Senseis, to ensure that their students achieve more than they do – as parents would for their own children – is truly the essence of what it means to be a Black Belt Sensei.

Section Ten

Power

We Are What We Can Imagine

Lesson Thirty-One

The Circle of Respect

All accomplished martial artists reflect on their past and how fortunate they are to have had a learned Sensei as their mentor. The common thread, woven into the fabric of all passionately dedicated teachers, is respect from – and for – their students. A "circle of respect" is created when students learn to respect their teachers, their teacher's teacher, and each other, for the gift of the martial arts.

> In order to receive respect, students must first be willing to give respect.

In order to receive respect, students must first be willing to give respect. Overt actions, such as public bowing and formal reference, are the usual manifestations. Genuine verbal expressions of respect are cherished by both students and teachers. Students display the enlightened quality of "emptiness" by putting their teacher "above them" despite the inevitable inequities that evolve, over time, regarding physical or mental adeptness.

Teachers, in an effort to ensure that their students accomplish more than they do, revel in their students' successes. Teachers and students come into conflict with, and ultimately surrender, their individual egos.

It is essential to this "circle of respect" that students avoid the pitfall of "growing out of themselves." All too often, students abandon their teacher and their own ideals in this relationship because their egos expand and overtake their better judgment. Students need to avoid this trap of self-glorification, in which they come to believe that their skills, knowledge, and wisdom surpass those of their teacher.

> Students eventually come to the realization that, despite their own hard work and dedication, who they are as martial artists has been determined by the person their teacher was or is.

Students eventually come to the realization that, despite their own hard work and dedication, who they are as martial artists has been determined by the person their teacher was or is. They have been shaped and encouraged by a caring mentor.

Sincere teachers will never expect outward displays of respect and will reject frivolous and unnecessary pageantry. They long to feel that their students respect them for the "gift" they have given. Respect is conveyed from student to teacher both directly – by friendship, dedication, and love of the art – and indirectly by their own students.

Nothing is felt so deeply and reverently as an expression of true respect, as when, for example, your student's disciples unconditionally value and trust your skills as a mentor. When your student's disciples demonstrate an eagerness to learn from you – because of what has been shared by their teacher – indirect but powerful respect is shared and appreciated.

Respect your teacher! Teach your students to respect your teacher through your teaching! Share the wisdom of this respect by your actions, as you, too, will have students who will contribute to this "circle of respect."

Be respectful – and you, in turn, will be respected!

Lesson Thirty-Two

The Mastery of Creative Thinking

Ingrained in human nature is a steadfast desire to be kind and gentle to other human beings. This good-natured outlook on life reflects the unconditioned childlike mind, free of prejudice and hatred, that dwells within all of us.

> The limitless boundaries of the imagination offer practitioners a very powerful tool for self-control.

Competing with our innate desire to be kind and compassionate is our "conditioned" self. Life experiences, traditions, belief systems and environmental influences contribute to life's maturation process, often making our kind, child-like nature more difficult to readily tap into. Herein resides the value of creative imagery.

As martial artists, we are trained and often called upon to:

> Become calm and control ourselves during times of excessive stress and anxiety. We must suppress or control feelings of anger in an effort to express kindness and compassion.

> Summon passion and violent emotion in order to defend life and limb. In response to an aggressive physical attack, we must gather the force necessary to subdue an opponent.

This dichotomy of emotional expression requires imaginative thinking and creativity!

Students may imagine a variety of mental images from actual or fictional circumstances that help to generate either "rage," such as a child being stolen from a mother, or "calm," such as a quiet moment near a serene mountain lake. This imagery is a form of creative thinking that conjures up a full-blown, parallel physiologic response.

> Learn to apply the techniques of creative imagery to create drama for your forms, energy and passion for your self-defense, and tranquil resolve for your anger and anxiety.

The limitless boundaries of the imagination offer practitioners a very powerful tool for self-control. Strive diligently to emphasize the power of the creative mind with your students. We are what we can imagine!

Use your creative thinking to define the focus and direction of your life's passion. Learn to apply the techniques of creative imagery to create drama for your forms, energy and passion for your self-defense, and tranquil resolve for your anger and anxiety.

Transcend the boundaries of your mind. The limits are what you decide them to be. Use imagery!

Lesson Thirty-Three

The Path to Peace Begins with Kindness

Every day of our existence, we encounter and are forced to endure conflict in one way or another. It is a reality of life that we have come to accept as part of all human relationships.

We are in charge of our thoughts. We can always choose the approach we take and the demeanor we present during difficult interpersonal interactions.

Dr. Terrence Webster-Doyle, in one of his wonderful Martial Arts for Peace books[1], illustrates this point beautifully. He tells an age-old Zen story in which three students are given the challenge of passing through a narrow rock canyon guarded by a wild stallion.

The first student approaches the stallion "head on," blocking and parrying the horse's attacks until eventually reaching the safety of the far side of the canyon. The teacher congratulates this student for exceptional strength and endurance.

The second student approaches the entrance and, upon encountering the stallion, decides to climb the walls of the canyon just above the reach of the attacking horse. This student successfully reaches the end of the canyon, avoiding the sharp hooves of the pursuing stallion. The teacher praises this student's ingenuity and cleverness.

The third student, after observing the strength of the first student and the cleverness of the second, walks cautiously to the entrance of the canyon and sits down on the ground. The student begins to play, like a child, with the abundant dirt and rocks, making gentle patterns in the soil. As the student plays peacefully on the floor of the canyon, the curious stallion approaches from behind. The kind and child-like demeanor of the student prompts a friendly encounter from this once aggressive horse. The student then stands and mounts the stallion, riding safely to the far end of the canyon.

---

[1] "Eye of the Hurricane," *Tales of the Empty-Handed Masters*, by Dr. Terrence Webster-Doyle. Atrium Society Publications, 1992.

This wonderfully illustrative story reveals three common approaches to conflict: A direct approach exhibiting strength and endurance; a clever approach in which one avoids and ignores; and an approach of peaceful resolve, where conflict is met with a child-like kindness.

As the story demonstrates, all three methods of approaching conflict may ultimately be successful. As intelligent martial artists our goal is always, first and foremost, the peaceful resolution of conflict. Achieving this goal requires all of these ingredients – strength, endurance, cleverness and peaceful resolve.

Persevere martial artists! Take control of your thoughts to create peace. Your attitudes and behaviors will follow. Embrace the paradox of the martial arts!

Discover for yourself how martial arts are truly a path to peace. When kindness prevails, humane living triumphs!

Go placidly amid the noise and haste, and remember what peace there may be in silence. As far as possible without surrender, be on good terms with all persons. Speak your truth quietly and clearly; and listen to others, even the dull and ignorant; they too have a story.

Avoid loud and aggressive persons, they are vexations of the spirit. If you compare yourself with others, you may become vain and bitter; for always there will be greater and lesser persons than yourself. Enjoy your achievements as well as your plans.

Keep interested in your own career, however humble; it is a real possession in the changing fortunes of time. Exercise caution in your business affairs, for the world is full of trickery. But let this not blind you to what virtue there is; many persons strive for high ideals, and everywhere life is full of heroism.

Be yourself. Especially, do not feign affection. Neither be cynical of love; for the face of all aridity and disenchantment is as perennial as the grass.

Take kindly the counsel of the years, gracefully surrendering the things of youth. Nurture strength of spirit to shield you in sudden misfortune, but do not distress yourself with imaginings. Many fears are born of fatigue and loneliness. Beyond a wholesome disciple, be gentle with yourself.

You are a child of the universe, no less than the trees and stars; you have a right to be here. And whether or not it is clear to you, no doubt the universe is unfolding as it should.

Therefore be at peace with God, whatever you conceive him or her to be; and whatever your labors and aspirations, and the noise and confusion of life, keep peace with your soul.

With all its sham, drudgery and broken dreams, it is still a beautiful world. Be careful. Strive to be happy.

– Anonymous
Old St. Paul's Church, 1692

To order additional copies of this book, visit
www.chaospublishing.com